I0755947

FINISHING LINE PRESS
www.finishinglinepress.com

The Well

a poem in nine parts by

Glen P. Vecchione

Finishing Line Press
Georgetown, Kentucky

The Well

ISBN 979-8-89990-478-3 First Edition

ACKNOWLEDGMENTS

With gratitude to Jan Parker, Karen Sleeth, Trish Sheppard and the Wildacres writing community of North Carolina.

Publisher: Leah Huete de Maines
Editor: Christen Kincaid
Cover Art and Design: Glen P. Vecchione
Author Photo: Glen P. Vecchione

Order online: www.finishinglinepress.com
also available on amazon.com

Author inquiries and mail orders:
Finishing Line Press
PO Box 1626
Georgetown, Kentucky 40324
USA

Contents

I. prairie fire 1

II. a sickness 3

III. the farm 5

IV. intruder 8

V. a bath 10

VI. two graves 12

VII. reasons 14

VIII. a prairie wind 15

IX. returning 16

in memoriam
Judy Tresino Parker 1945-1970
J. Louise Wheeler 1945-2014

I. Prairie Fire

Sestina Rigida

It was a hoodoo moon and pinochle behind the old barn
among hired farmhands who swore and drank too much,
a farm gone shoddy since Willaert lost his wife and young daughter
to a strange, shivering heat brought on by some filth in the well.
So, he went to bed early and let the men do as they pleased.
They did as they pleased: mocking his sullen oddness in the dark

yard after the house lights sputtered, pitching their cards across dark
grass until, one night, one of them brought kerosine from the barn.
But the lanterns were damaged, and their sooty burn didn't please
these gamblers (who couldn't tell spades from diamonds), so a much
bolder thing was done—an open fire, hootch-kindled, by a well
dug in the southern prairie between two large farms. The daughter

of a neighbor saw it through her window. Lars Dinssen's daughter
Elyssia ran to her parents' bedroom as flames cleaved the dark
outside, reddening the walls. Before father Dinssen was well
awake, mother Dinssen sprung up, shouting: "Calves in barn!"
and "Damnable commotion!" But Elyssia Dinssen was pleased
to show this intelligence: they must stay in the house—that much

was certain—stay in the night-cool house where they'd be much
safer from fast-moving prairie fire. A brave, clever daughter,
she tore down the curtains teasing, "Now this should please
you, father: a good light to read by when you're up after dark!"
But soon the leaping fire made a cyclone behind the barn,
and it was time to flee. There was one hope: the abandoned well.

Flames licked as they stumbled through clotheslines to the well.
Mother Dinssen began to climb down, but the rope-hemp was much
too worn to hold her and it snapped. She tumbled, broad as a barn
down that narrow shaft, splashing when she hit bottom. Daughter
and father knew the shallow well and jumped the dark
maw fearlessly—scraping knees against rough walls before the pleas

of calves made flesh crawl. Dinssen looked up: "Lord, please
spare my calves!" he choked; "Poor innocents, keep them well!"
begged his wife—a plain prayer from plain people knee-deep in dark
slime that stank of death. *There had to be more than this, much
more than this harsh life of toil, of pain, of grief—father, daughter,
mother, asleep in bed before that red ball behind the barn.*

Lars Dinssen's daughter wept with her parents. There was much
to lose: house, good crops, solid barn with calves—all hung on a dark
plea to assuage something quick and cruel from a black well.

II. A Sickness

One week of the barn laid bare: a burn-crumpled roof
atop rafters like a smoldering ribcage that fouled
the air and made them cover their faces when crossing
the yard to feed the pigs. Their house, intact but singed,
banked high as a gewgawed hat against a hellscape
of charred cottonwood and hourglass-shaped eddies
thick with the down-fruiting of dandelion purr

so that the whole of the southern acreage was combed
with ash, and from uncurtained windows in the sickroom,
a view of the dead-burn spread out like a ghostly handprint
in the shortgrass, thick at the wrist and traceable backwards
along the forearm to Willaert's farm where there was nothing
much in the way of damage.

The well, too, stood stalwart in the charred prairie,
a useless acre that Dinssen and Willaert both claimed but
neither had used, each building a fence that the other tore down.
Years ago, they'd shared the well as neighbors, but Willaert
soured after he took a wife, and the cruel woman plated it over.

But now the wife was dead along with their child, and Willaert,
turned repentant but bitter, opened the well and proclaimed
the water safe, although few believed him.
Repentant but bitter, that's how Dinssen saw him—a man
secretly vengeful as he'd lost what was most dear to him
and, being godless, required an enemy.

For three days Lars Dinssen stood in the ruins of his farm
long after dark, until one night, as a crescent moon sharpened
its blade over the burned animals, he whispered in his own ear,
I will go down and kill Willaert.
And in the morning, as his wife coughed blood into a knurl of fist,
he drew out the long rifle from under their bed.
"He done this?" said wife, "Serves you right. Killing him won't make
the water good, but 'tis true I thirst, so go fetch me some."

I will go down and kill Willaert. Elyssia will stay with you.
But daughter would not stay, hoping to ease his murderous resolve
as they walked to the undamaged property of a hated neighbor.
She would not stay, and seeing her stubbornness, he knew
he would either take her or abandon what his heart demanded.
So, he took her.

III. The Farm

Pantoum

The grass whistled, cutting against his trouser legs.
He strode hugely—rifle hard against his shoulder
and glanced back only once at his stumbling daughter
who knew much better than to speak to him just then.

He strode hugely—rifle hard against his shoulder
and tromped through the fields well ahead of his daughter
who knew much better than to speak to him just then,
stumbling behind in her long skirt, blouse unbuttoned.

He tromped through the burned fields ahead of his daughter,
a speck of a man now, against Willaert's great barn.
Stumbling behind in her long dress, blouse unbuttoned,
she finally called out to him and he waited,

a speck of a man now, against Willaert's great barn,
both at the blackened pit where the fire began.
She finally called out to him and he waited
in the silo shade, sifting through charred playing cards,

both at the blackened pit where the fire began:
melted cups and broken whiskey bottles glinting
in the silo shade. Sifting through charred playing cards,
he found a small, silver coin flashing amid the

melted cups and shards of broken whiskey bottles.
Dropping it, he noticed Willaert's wagon was gone
and found another small coin flashing amid the
hasty wreckage of this scene—a strange, ill omen—

glinting in the sun, and saw that the wagon gone.
Elyssia saw the same: wagon gone, swinging door,
the hasty wreckage of this scene—strange, ill omens.
A silent farmhouse. "Something's wrong, father," she said.

Elyssia saw the same: wagon gone, swinging door
as they walked through each large room, watching for danger.
A silent farmhouse. "Something's wrong, father," she said.
"Perhaps he's hurt." Beneath hundreds of photographs,

they walked through each large room, watching for danger,
portraits of wife and daughter in vanished gardens.
Perhaps he *was* hurt. Hundreds of photographs—before
they saw the prone figure in the kitchen: Willaert,

beneath his wife and daughter in vanished gardens.
He was propped against the wall in a pool of blood.
They saw the prone figure in the kitchen. Willaert,
half his neck blown away, the gun thrown back from him.

He was propped against the wall in a pool of blood
(and there was Dinssen ready to use his rifle),
half his neck blown away, the gun thrown back from him.
Dinssen felt an unmanly sorrow in his heart,

and foolish, so eager to use his own rifle
to punish a hated neighbor for the dread fire.
Dinssen felt an unmanly sorrow in his heart
and a huge sickness in the pit of his belly.

To punish a hated neighbor for the dread fire
when it was nothing but hired farmhands—foul men.
A huge sickness grew in the pit of his belly
while his daughter went straight to work, cleaning the blood.

When it was nothing but hired farmhands—foul men
drinking, setting fires, murdering, and then fleeing.
While his daughter went straight to work, cleaning the blood,
he swallowed his bitter vengeance and was ashamed.

Drinking, setting fires, murdering, and then fleeing—
he'd find every last foul farmhand and punish him.
He swallowed his bitter vengeance and was ashamed
until Elyssia spoke to him: "Leave me. Go out."

He'd find every last foul farmhand and punish him;
he knew this as he watched his child at her grim task.
Again, Elyssia spoke to him: "Leave me. Go out."
She wanted him in the barn to check the horses.

He knew this as he watched his child at her grim task,
glancing back at her only once as she stumbled.
She wanted him in the barn to check the horses.
The grass whistled, cutting against his trouser legs.

IV. Intruder

Under dry-rot joists and a slack-jawed crampon
the huge door wheeled open, clacking like a boxcar.
Inside, ladder bowed against ladder at the loft,
and timbered stables lined the sides, all empty.
A man could do well with a barn like this: the silo
tight-banded and braced against the listing tonnage,
the rafters tarred, the wide floor swept clean for
horses and livestock although Willaert kept only horses.

Where were they? Escaped? Stolen? Frightened
into the night as a fire bloomed behind them?
And no spare wagon nor wheel nor bit nor bridle?—
unless a tack-room hid behind that door just wide
enough for a man. But he found nothing there
in the way of stable gear: grass clumped along the flanks
of washtubs, knives and hatchets slotted neatly, long
strips of pigskin and rough-cut fur hardened, fat still attached.

Abattoir? Slaughter-room? But nothing alive here.
And no pigs nor hogs nor sheep nor rabbits?—
unless there was something else Willaert cut
to pieces in this secret chamber of his cavern-barn.

Dinssen shuddered. And what was it caused him to turn
and walk towards the bright square of door,
tightening his gun-grip? The cloudless sky blinded him
and he visored his eyes. Willaert's wagon, packed tight
with Willaert's prized geldings, vagrant in the harness chair
who yelled towards the farmhouse, cracking his road horses
into a panicked bolt, so that the wagon careened through the gate
with a ramshackle clatter and pitched down the road.
If there were two men, one was still inside.

His knuckles blanched as he squeezed the rifle
and entered the house, banging the screened door behind him.
He strode towards the kitchen and caught the man
in a black-toothed leer, stinking of liquor

as he steadied himself by the wall and wiped his groin.
On the floor, Elyssia: naked, save for feet where stockings
caught rills of blood. Elyssia: naked and frightened and ashamed
to be seen by both father and defiler—one in the other.
And in the instant before a rush of rage paralyzed him,
Dinssen raised his rifle and fired, blowing a dark rose
in the man's belly, so that smoke hung in the air, obscuring
a tangled knot of clothing thrown across the table.

V. A Bath

Sapphic Verse

A long moment passed before she rose and stood,
said nothing, but looked away from the horror.
Dinssen staggered forward, crashing into chairs,
grabbing his daughter

although he offered no comfort but only,
"Put on your clothes so we can leave this evil."
Shaking now, he stared through the window feeling
utterly helpless.

Briefly meeting rage in her eyes, he cupped her
face and rasped, "Cover your nakedness, daughter."
But she lurched forward, pushing his hands away,
screamed at him hoarsely,

"Stop it, father! How can I go before I've
flushed this snake venom from me
before it spreads throughout my body to root?
Leave me to bathe, please!"

Soiled, wretched, stinking of someone else, she
walked, nearly swooning, to the well in the prairie
wanting nothing more than to purge herself clean,
leach out the poison.

Wrapped in linen, walking without her slippers,
stumbling, cursing, straining to reach slaking stones,
climbing over, dropping down into darkness
and shamelessly nude,

she scooped the brackish well-water over her
body, clenched the rot-clotted coolness inside
splashed it against her face and shoulders, her
tightening nipples

stinking water, rubbed it roughly against her
soft belly. Then, cupping it deep within her,
she tried to draw out the swimming germ
from her body.

Dinssen watched her emerge in the dim dusk-light.
Elyssia: how harshly she'd scolded today!—
banished, sent to check on the stable horses,
foolishly leaving.

Enter a farmhand, taking pleasure crudely
just like an animal—*evil and vicious.*
Dinssen looked around for a shovel, finding
one in the cellar.

VI. Two Graves

There was nothing left to do but bury the bodies,
Willaert and his murderous farmhand.
First Willaert, nearer the house, dappled by the shadows
of a barren rose pergola,
then the farmhand in the barn beneath animal dung.

And the digging went quickly as the soil was soft.
Willaert in a deep-dug grave cut straight through the loam
so that the soil turned wet and clumped against the shovel,
sticking fast.

Dinssen dropped to his knees and touched the ground.
Water rose up to his knuckles.
With strong fingers, he raked the earthen floor dry
but it quickly glassed over again, more water rising.
Then he saw it: the clean white of a bone, or pair of bones,
joined at the end like a crossbow and as pliable.
Plucking it out, he found another bone, then another,
and as he continued to sift, he knew the soil was filled
with bone.

Dinssen walked back to the house and found
his daughter dressing. Avoiding her eyes, he hoisted
the farmhand over his shoulders and loped towards the barn,
remembering the slaughter-room.
Now this man deserved no flowerbed.
Beneath the stench of stretched skins he would lie,
crumpled like a butchered animal,
his clothes—an arsonist's clothes—burned to cinders.

But the digging was difficult here and the grave shallower.
Again, he hit water, and looking down,
he saw whorls of white like the fat from animals;
and when he thrust his hands down, his fingers
touched bone again—whole fistfuls of it—a wattle-fence
of bone stretching beneath the barn, he was sure of it,

and beyond the barn to fields and prairies, a cesspool of decay
whose wobbling eye flashed from the bottom of the well.

He covered the body carelessly,
desiring only to be finished and leave the place.
But as he scooped the last mound, a glint of light
from his spade signaled.
Looking closer, he recognized the remains of a beaded sleeve
and the tracery of slender bones, a human hand.
But what he saw inside that nexus chilled him:
a smaller hand, that of a child's, flesh still attached,
but the whole crumpled and crablike.

Dinssen threw down the shovel and strode from the barn.
It was time to journey back with Elyssia.
It was time to walk back through the shadowed fields to his farm.

VII. Reasons

Duodectet

There were reasons; a man always had his reasons—
Willaert's barn, Willaert's property, Willaert's secrets.
His wife and daughter dead from a fever, he'd heard.
But no wagon nor church-bell nor hymn from the choir?

There were reasons; a man always had his reasons—
The space dark and emptied of Willaert's strong horses.
Abattoir? Slaughter-room? But nothing alive here.
And no cattle nor hogs nor sheep nor rabbits?

If there were reasons, Dinssen would never know them
as surely there were reasons, and good ones, unknown
to neighbors; but why the bones and the tiny hand?
And why so many bones stretching beneath the fields?

Dinssen threw down the shovel and strode from the barn.
It was time to walk back to his house and safety.
A dull window light signaled she still lived, his wife,
although when he looked out again the light was gone.

Dinssen remembered she'd asked him for water
and how he pretended not to hear the request
but fetched it for her all the same without speaking.
And why would she ask when she knew it was poisoned?

There are reasons; a man always has his reasons
he'd thought, lifting the tin cup to his wife's pale lips
as his daughter gasped and turned so she wouldn't see
when he forced her mother to gulp and to swallow.

His wife would never know the reason for his kindness.
And, when gone, they would slowly put right the ruined farm,
Dinssen and his daughter. They would prepare for frost
then sleep back-to-belly as lovers by firelight.

VIII. A Prairie Wind

A gale came up and rattled the trees, startling crows.
Shadows pooled alongside the fenceposts as the sun
burned down to ember, and clouds, like cuttlebones,
signaled the way back.

Elyssia said nothing, her hair blown into a shredded rag.
But when he touched her, she jumped away and grabbed
between her legs, whimpering like a child.
Then she turned to him, face flushed and eyes gleaming
in the way of something hard and bitter that quickly
throws back what settles onto it.

He drew her near and stroked her hair, twisted strands
between his fingers—his coarse fingers—then remembered
the touch of bone and pulled his hand away.
He thought, for an instant, that she reached out to take his hand,
but if so, she quickly withdrew again behind feral eyes.

They would go home to supper, both exhausted.
They would sit together around the table,
father and frightened daughter.

IX. Returning

Palindrome

"Say nothing, nothing of today,
and look away from here, Elyssia—forever.
We'll eat, then sit beside the fire in our own house.
You'll say nothing of today to your mother."
His voice was coarse

for she staggered far behind him,
gripping herself strangely,
as they made their way back
under a purpling sky
through a landscape they could hardly recognize now:
burned cascades of wild oak and jug-shaped wasp nests,
singed fruit in a long orchard.

He asked again:
"Does it pain so badly
that I should I leave you and find a doctor?"

But she shivered piteously and he could do nothing.
How could he comfort her?—
What was the secret poultice of fatherhood?—
He did not understand daughters, nor wives;
they talked in a language he did not speak.

A man knows his seasons:
he plots his acreage,
he plans the harvesting he'll enjoy as a young farmer
and learns the practical labors of husband and father;
he sells what he cannot eat and buys an automobile
and soon hires men like his younger self.

A man knows his seasons:
if without a son he looks to his men for a man,
watching him turn the soil as he himself once did;
he gives away his automobile and walks to church alone;

he sleeps with warmth in his belly and death for his coverlet.
And if a man is betrayed, ruined, and ridiculed,
he takes his life or the life of his betrayer and is forgiven.

But as for the women of men:
they hold mysteries, being more of the air than the earth.
Easily broken, they are cut down in the full of their stride.
For reasons unknowable, disconnected from soil but for its water
moving up into them and then out again.

And as for the women of men:
they are temperament and imagination,
succumbing to the plague of their kind, nervousness.
Although they are honest and hardworking, a man might avoid
thinking too much of their storms and passions,
their melancholy;
and if a woman enjoys too much the pleasures
of a man's body, he should be wary of it lest she
distract him and fall into fever,
as in Leviticus:
Your strength spent in vain and your land not yield its increase.

"Elyssia!"
Dinssen wiped his face, stretching it strangely.
"Stop it now or tell me to find a doctor. You're a grown woman!"
She turned from him, covering her ears.
"A grown woman who soon enough would've known a man.
We survive, we survive.
A grown woman who soon enough would've known a man."
She turned from him, covering her ears.
"Stop it now or tell me to find a doctor. You're a grown woman!"
Dinssen wiped his face, stretching it strangely.
"Elyssia!"

Your strength spent in vain and your land not yield its increase,
as in Leviticus.

Distracted, she fell into a fevered
dread of a man's body, and he was wary of it.
For if a woman fears too much those pleasures
she will be melancholy
and think only of her storms and passions.
Although his daughter was honest and hardworking, she was
succumbing to the plague of all women: nervousness,
temperament and imagination.
For women have their men

to move up into them and then out again.
For reasons unknowable, disconnected from soil but for its water.
Easily broken, they are cut down in the full of their stride
but hold mysteries, being more of the air than the earth.
These are the women of men.

A man may take his life or the life of a betrayer and be forgiven
if he is betrayed, ruined, and ridiculed.
He sleeps with warmth in his belly and death for his coverlet.
He gives away his automobile and walks to church alone.
Watching another man turn the soil as he himself once did,
he chooses that man from among his men,
a man who also knows his seasons,

who soon hires men like his younger self
and sells what he cannot eat to buy another automobile;
who learns the practical labors of husband and father
and plans the harvesting he'll enjoy as a young farmer:
plotting his acreage according to season.

They spoke a language he did not speak,
daughters and wives, and could not understand.
What was the secret poultice of fatherhood?—
How could he comfort her?—
She shivered piteously and he could do nothing.
"Should I leave you and find a doctor

that it pains so badly?"
he asked again.

Singed fruit in a long orchard,
burned cascades of wild oak and jug-shaped wasp nests—
a landscape they could hardly recognize now
under a purpling sky
as they made their way back,
she staggering far behind him,
gripping herself strangely.

His voice was coarse:
"You'll say nothing of today to your mother.
We'll eat, then sit beside the fire in our own house.
Look away from here, Elyssia—forever.
Say nothing, nothing of today."

Glen Vecchione, who also writes under the name Glen Peters, is the author of 28 commercial science, math, and history books that have been translated into several languages and distributed throughout the world. His poetry appears in *Prairie Schooner, Penn Review, ZYZZYVA* (1997), *Chautauqua Review* (2024), *Comstock Review* (2022), and *Main Street Rag* (2021). Glen, who studied under the poet and critic Douglas Fiero at UCLA, won the 2023 Editor's Choice Award in *Last Stanza Journal* and was the featured poet in *Sequestrum*'s "Wonder" issue, January 2024.

Glen comes to poetry and fiction-writing from a variety of other careers—actor, composer for film and television, and playwright. In 1980, Glen wrote the music and lyrics to the Broadway Jazz Ballet *The Legend of Frankie and Johnny*, produced by the Nat Horne Dance Theatre of New York. His play-in-verse, *Cowboy BO and the Train Whistle* was produced at the Lyceum Theatre in San Diego in 2011. Glen currently divides his time between the California desert and Umbria, Italy—his "go to" place for developing new ideas. His first novel, *Where the Nights Smell Like Bread*, was released in April 2025 and is the first of many pieces that will explore his life as a half-year resident of a foreign country. His second novel *The Crows*, was released in April 2026 and a memoir, *Fire Exit*, is scheduled for release in 2027. *(https://glenvecchione.com)*

www.ingramcontent.com/pod-product-compliance
Lightning Source LLC
LaVergne TN
LVHW090542110826
845146LV00003B/1238

* 9 7 9 8 8 9 9 9 0 4 7 8 3 *